Survival Jobs Directory
New York Edition

Michelle Dyer

Table of Contents

Preface:

I can still remember sitting on the floor of AEA asking friends for temp agency recommendations. "Why isn't there a resource out there to help us find a Survival Job?" I thought. So, I created one.

www.SurvivalJobsForActors.com

Inside you'll find a directory of over 70 companies that hire actors for Survival Jobs and the details on how to apply. Each industry is different, so I'll include notes if there's anything else that might be helpful to know.

Please let employers know where you heard about their company – the more they hear about us, the more jobs they will send us for you!

Thanks so much for your support. I hope this directory helps you find tons of wonderful gigs to help you pay the rent while you follow your dreams. I know it was sure made with a lot of love.

Best wishes on your Survival Job journey – and please keep in touch via Social Media.

http://twitter.com/SurvivalJobs
http://www.facebook.com/SurvivalJobsForActors
http://www.youtube.com/user/SurvivalJobs4Actors

All the best,
Michelle Dyer

4

What do I say?

When it says "email your resume to" that also means including a note in the body of the email. Just don't blindly send out emails with attachments.

Include a paragraph introducing yourself, tell them where you found out about their company, and mention any experience you may have in that area.

For a temp agency I might write:

Dear Maria,

I would like to submit my resume for temp work at The Supporting Cast. I heard about your company from Michelle Dyer/ Survival Jobs for Actors.

My past office temp experience includes reception work, meeting and greeting guests, and processing expenses. Please see attached for my resume.

I would like the opportunity to meet you and become a valuable member of The Supporting Cast team. Feel free to contact me at (917) 737-1222 or SurvivalJobsForActors@gmail.com.

Best regards,

Michelle Dyer

The Big Interview

Interviews are different for each company. For a temp job, you're going to have a more formal interview than for a promo gig. You probably won't wear a suit to a promo interview, but don't look like you've just rolled out of bed either. Employers want to see you at your best.

Never arrive more than 10 minutes early, but DO NOT be late. Most offices in New York City have security desks in the lobby, so leave yourself some extra time in case there's a line at the sign-in desk.

Bring at least 2 hard copies of your resume (and a few pictures if you're going to a promo interview.) The employer will probably open the conversation with "tell me a little about yourself," so have about 30 seconds prepared.

(example) "I moved to New York in 2002 to pursue musical theatre. In between gigs, I've been doing office temp and promo work. I really enjoy interacting with the public in promo work, so that's why I'm looking for another promo company to work with."

Do a little research – that's why I included the website and social media links for each company. It's always good to have one or two short questions about the company or job prepared. Interviewers like asking "Do you have any questions for me?"

Is the company socially savvy? If your interview with a socially savvy promo company went really well, you might want to give them a mention on your way home. "Just had a great interview with @GCMarketing – look forward to working together!"

Most employers love actors, because they're typically outgoing and charismatic; so feel free to breathe, relax and be yourself. Be honest with the commitment you are willing to give (whether you want to do one day temp jobs, or jobs that last a week.) You want to gain trust with your temp agent or promo manager. You probably won't get the most desirable gigs to begin with, but if you shine like a star and have a great attitude and work ethic on not-so-fun ones, you'll become their go-to guy or gal when that choice gig comes up.

Your Business Resume

Most companies want to see a business resume. This includes all non-acting gigs you have worked.

Most of the employers I talk to want your resume as a Word Document (for my Mac users, make sure you make it a .doc document – NOT .doc**x,** which it will auto-default to if you don't specify in the drop-down when you first save it.) It's also good to save your resume as a pdf as well. (File -> Save As -> Pull down the "Format" button to "PDF")

Don't have a business resume yet? Check out the Survival Jobs' blog post for a template you can use:

http://www.survivaljobsforactors.com/o-res-u-me

* Notice all of the action verbs – Answered, Generated, Scheduled, Updated – use them.

* NEVER lie. That should go without saying.

Don't think you have any skills that translate into the "real" work world?

　　　* How about providing excellent customer service?

　　　* Thinks fast on his/her feet (Improv anyone?)

　　　* Easily adapts to change

　　　* Strong computer skills – Mac and/or PC

　　　* Great communication skills

How many companies do I work with?

You might not click with every single temp agent, promo company, or catering company that you interview with. I interviewed with at least five temp agencies when I was starting out, and only one or two called me for jobs.

I say, register with as many companies as you can. In the interview ask how they'd like you to keep them updated on your availability. Most like a weekly email. So, just keep in touch with a quick and friendly email informing them of your availability for the next week (I liked to send mine on a Thursday) and when an opportunity comes up that you are right for, you will be fresh on their mind (and in their Inbox.)

And now... on to the listings!

Promotional Work:

Have you ever seen people standing outside Penn Station handing out samples of a new product? That's a promo gig.

Promotional work usually consists of handing out samples, or demoing a product for the public. Many companies use the phrase "brand ambassador." The best people for promos are friendly, outgoing individuals that love to interact with the public.

Usually the promo company will ask for your picture and a resume– it's like a modeling gig, but you have to talk. Smiley pictures are always best to submit. Let your personality shine through in the interview.

You can register with as many promo companies as you like. They will all have different gigs that they need to find great promo people for. Sometimes the client will give feedback on each promo person, so be sure to be professional at all times during the gig. From time to time the client will request someone that they have worked with before, because they liked them so much.

Most of the time you'll get a t-shirt or outfit from the promo company to wear during the gig. Look polished and professional – from your nails to your freshly ironed outfit.

Women – for makeup usually err on the side of conservative. If it's a nightlife promo, that's when you can do a more nighttime look.

In the world of promos – Image is everything.

360 Events & Promotions

Phone: (858) 748-6360
Website: http://www.360promonetwork.com

How to apply:
> Email 3 photos, a resume with work experience, and your contact information to:
> bookings@360promonetwork.com

Advice from 360: "We like clean cut photos. Something more conservative."

http://twitter.com/360Promos
http://www.facebook.com/360Promos
http://www.linkedin.com/company/360-events-&-promotions

Attack!

Phone: (917) 289-1074
Website: http://www.attackmarketing.net

How to apply:
Online - Click on "Talent Registration"
on the top right of the page:
http://www.attackmarketing.net/login.ph
p

http://twitter.com/AttackMarketing
http://twitter.com/AttackThisGig
http://www.facebook.com/attackmarketing
http://www.linkedin.com/company/98917
http://www.youtube.com/user/attackmarketing
vids

Awestruck

Phone: (212) 381-9500
Website: http://www.getawestruck.com

How to apply:
> Email a picture and resume to:
> promos@getawestruck.com

http://twitter.com/awestruckmktg
http://www.facebook.com/awestruckmarketing
http://www.linkedin.com/company/2389183?tr
k=tyah

Brand Allure Staff

(aka SOZA Model Management & Event
Staffing)
Phone: (646) 201-4875
Website: http://brandallurestaff.com

How to apply:
> Online at:
> http://brandallurestaff.com/apply-to-
> brandallure-models.php

Note from Survival Jobs: Brand Allure is also
owned by SOZA, so you just have to apply on
the Brand Allure site above.

http://twitter.com/BrandAllureInc
http://www.linkedin.com/company/brand-
allure-inc.

CTI Convention Staffing

Phone : (212) 297-1211
Website: http://www.cticonventionstaffing.com

How to apply:
    Call (212) 297-1211 to see when the
    next group interview session will be
    held. If no one is there, leave a
    message with your name, contact info,
    how you heard about them, and any
    event experience you may have.

Note from Survival Jobs: Hence the name,
this company does staffing for conventions –
most of the positions are the people who
register you, hand out badges, give directions,
etc.

Elite Marketing Group

Phone: (212) 933-9544 x200
Website: http://www.elitemg.com

How to apply:
Online at:
http://www.elitemg.com//contact_promotional.cfm

http://www.facebook.com/pages/Elite-Marketing-Group/111103918930606
http://www.linkedin.com/company/elite-marketing-group

Encore Nationwide

Phone: 1-866-438-7823
Website: http://www.encorenationwide.com

How to apply:
Online at:
http://www.encorenationwide.com (You have to click on "Sign-up today" and then "Click here to become part of the Encore Talent Team.")

http://twitter.com/encorenw
http://www.facebook.com/pages/Encore-Nationwide/105083416193924
http://www.linkedin.com/company/encore-nationwide

EventPro Strategies

Phone: (480) 449-4100
Website: http://eventprostrategies.com

How to apply:
 http://eventprostrategies.com/talent/over
 view

http://twitter.com/eventpro
http://www.facebook.com/eventstaffing
http://www.linkedin.com/company/eventpro-
strategies
http://www.youtube.com/user/EventProStrateg
ies1

Fusion Event Staffing

Phone: (678) 762-1113
Website: http://www.fusioneventstaffing.com

How to apply:
Online at:
https://www.fusiongateway.com/apply/register.cfm

https://twitter.com/FusionEventStaf
http://www.facebook.com/FusionEventStaffing
http://www.linkedin.com/company/fusion-event-staffing
http://www.youtube.com/user/FusionEventStaffing

GC Marketing Services

Phone: (212) 780-5200
Website: http://www.gcmarketingservices.com

How to apply:
>Online at:
>http://login.gcmarketingservices.com/frontend/register.php

Note from Survival Jobs: GC Marketing has a great blog full of tips for applying and working promo gigs. Be sure to check it out.

http://twitter.com/gcmarketing
http://www.facebook.com/gcmarketingservices
http://www.linkedin.com/company/gc-marketing-services
http://www.youtube.com/user/GCMarketingServices
https://plus.google.com/117084252108271486735/posts

GO GORILLA
Phone: (212) 925-2420
Website: http://www.gogorillamedia.com

How to apply:
> Go to http://www.gogorillaadvertising.com/Careers.aspx and click on the "Talent" button. That should open up an email to info@gogorillamedia.com where you can send your resume and headshot.

http://twitter.com/gogorillamedia
http://www.facebook.com/gogorilla
http://www.linkedin.com/company/gogorilla-media
http://www.youtube.com/user/gogorillamediadotcom

The Michael Alan Group

Phone: (212) 563-7656
Website: http://www.michael-alan.com

How to apply:
> "We ask that people submit their headshots and resumes with any referral information to info@michael-alan.com with Promotional Staffer Submission in the subject."

http://twitter.com/magmarketing
http://www.facebook.com/pages/The-Michael-Alan-Group/151724584887003
http://www.linkedin.com/company/the-michael-alan-group
http://www.youtube.com/user/themichaelalangroup

Spectrum Events

Website: http://www.spectrum-events.net

How to apply:
Online at: http://www.spectrum-events.net/talentsubmission2.html

http://twitter.com/Spectrum_Events
http://www.facebook.com/pages/Spectrum-Events-Inc/139760508001

Victory Marketing Agency

Phone: (239) 332-7392
Website: http://www.victory-agency.com

How to apply:
   Fill out the "Contact Us" form at
http://www.victory-agency.com.

http://twitter.com/VictoryMktg
http://www.facebook.com/VictoryMarketing

Victory Models & Event Staffing

Phone: (917) 455-0870
Website: http://victory-models.com

How to apply:
Email your headshot and resume to:
model@victory-models.com

http://twitter.com/VictoryModels
http://www.facebook.com/victorymodels

Broadway Promotional Work:

Most Broadway promo jobs are handing out
flyers for the shows. Actors are ideal for this
job, because they are enthusiastic and
knowledgeable about theatre. Some jobs
make an hourly rate, and some make base
plus commission.

aka New York

Phone: (212) 584-0400
Website: http://www.akanyc.net

How to apply:
Email your headshot and resume to:
broadwaypromos@gmail.com

http://twitter.com/aka_NewYorkCity
http://www.facebook.com/akaNewYorkCity
http://www.youtube.com/akanewyorkcity

Davenport Theatrical

Phone: (212) 874-5348
Website: http://www.davenporttheatrical.com

How to apply:
> Email your headshot, resume, and any sales/promotions experience to: streetteam@davenporttheatrical.com

Note from Survival Jobs: You can work as much or as little as you want. This job is usually commission only, so they usually ask you to apply only if you have an iPhone or Droid (so you can process ticket sales on the street with your phone.)

Teams on Broadway
(HHC Marketing)
Phone: (212) 840-3335
Website: http://www.hhcmarketing.com

How to apply:
> Email your headshot and resume to:
> BwyPromo@gmail.com

Note from Survival Jobs: Teams on Broadway is the street team company for HHC Marketing.

theatreMAMA

Phone: (212) 581-5863
Website: http://www.theatremama.com

How to apply:
      Email your headshot and performing resume to: auditions@theatremama.com. Bring in business resume if you have an interview.

http://www.facebook.com/GOMAMA
http://twitter.com/nyctheatre
http://vimeo.com/theatremama
http://www.linkedin.com/company/theatremama

Type A Marketing

Phone: (212) 307-0800
Website: http://www.typeamktg.com

How to apply:
>   Send your resume to
>   info@typeamktg.com with "Brand
>   Ambassador" in the subject line.

http://twitter.com/typeamktg
http://www.facebook.com/pages/Type-A-
Marketing/171157782895756

Catering/Events:

You'll need a pair of black pants, a black or white button-up shirt, and a very comfortable pair of black shoes. Some companies will ask you to provide your own tux as well.

If you need a tux or tie check out:

O.K. Uniform Company
253 Church St.
New York, NY 10013
Phone: 1-866-700-5765

Abigail Kirsch

Phone: (914) 631-3030
Website: http://www.abigailkirsch.com

How to apply:
Email your resume to:
caterwaiters@abigailkirsch.com.

Notes from Survival Jobs: Abigail Kirsch is the exclusive caterer for Pier Sixty at Chelsea Piers, The New York Botanical Garden, among others. Zagat rated them as a top caterer in New York City and they're known for high-end weddings.

http://twitter.com/abigailkirsch
http://www.facebook.com/abigailkirschcatering
http://www.linkedin.com/company/abigail-kirsch

Amerivents

Phone: (212) 245-1080
Website: http://www.amerivents.com

How to apply:
    Online at:
    http://www.amerivents.com/talent

Note from Survival Jobs: Scott usually staffs the US Open each year, which is at the end of the summer at the USTA Billie Jean King National Tennis Center in Queens.

http://twitter.com/Amerivents
http://www.facebook.com/pages/Amerivents/1 14970265250044

Book Your Staff

Phone: (917) 881-6877
Website: http://bookyourstaff.com

How to apply:
Online at:
http://bookyourstaff.com/employment.html

byDavid

Phone: (212) 722-8705
Website: http://www.bydavidnyc.com

How to apply:
    Email your headshot and resume to:
    victoria@bydavidnyc.com.

Choice Productions

Phone: (212) 265-5012
Website: http://choiceproductionsnyc.com

How to apply:
  Email your resume to:
  jenna@choiceproductionsnyc.com.

http://twitter.com/choiceeventsnyc
http://www.facebook.com/pages/Choice-
Productions-NYC/44913445252
http://www.linkedin.com/company/choice-
productions
http://www.youtube.com/user/ChoiceProductio
nsNYC

Creative Edge Parties

Phone: (212) 741-3000
Website: http://www.creativeedgeparties.com

How to apply:
> Email your picture and resume to:
> Gilleon@creativeedgeparties.com.

Note from Survival Jobs: The Roundabout Theatre Company usually uses Creative Edge for their Galas.

http://twitter.com/creativeedgenyc
http://www.facebook.com/CreativeEdgePartie s
http://www.linkedin.com/company/creative-edge-parties

Decorum Consulting Group

Phone: (212) 679-7272
Website: http://www.decorum-ny.com

How to apply:
Email your resume to:
tobia@decorum-ny.com.

Great Performances

Phone: (212) 727-2424
Website: http://www.greatperformances.com

How to apply:
>   Email your resume to:
>   careers@greatperformances.com

https://twitter.com/GPfood
http://www.facebook.com/GPFood
http://www.linkedin.com/company/great-performances

Model Bartenders and Premier Party Servers

Phone: (212) 499-0886
Website: http://www.modelbartenders.com

How to apply:
> Email your photo and resume to:
> info@modelbartenders.com.

Note from Survival Jobs: Model Bartenders is the same company as Premier Party Servers. When you submit your photo and resume, you're applying to both places.

http://www.facebook.com/modelbartenders

Neuman's

Phone: (212) 228-2444
Website: http://www.caterernyc.com

How to apply:
    Email your resume and a headshot to
    Amanda: aweidel@caterernyc.com

http://twitter.com/neumansnyc
http://www.facebook.com/NeumansCatering
http://www.linkedin.com/company/neuman%27s-catering

NOVA Catering and Events

Phone: (212) 977-8900
Website: http://www.novacateringco.com

How to apply:
    Email your resume to:
    info@novacateringco.com

http://www.linkedin.com/company/nova-catering

Open Bar Hospitality and Greenlight Events

Phone: (212) 736-1119
Website: http://www.openbarhospitality.com

How to apply:
Email your headshot and resume to:
info@greenlightevents.com

Note from Survival Jobs: When you send in your information to the email above, you're applying for both Open Bar and Greenlight.

http://www.facebook.com/pages/Open-Bar-Hospitality/224080641014412

Prime Events Inc.

Phone: (732) 784-7545
Website: http://www.primeeventsinc.com

How to apply:
>   Email your picture and resume to:
>   jobs@primeeventsinc.com

http://twitter.com/PRIMEeventsNYC
http://www.facebook.com/PRIMEeventsInc
http://www.linkedin.com/company/prime-events-inc

Scoozi Events

Phone: (212) 799-0080
Website: http://www.scoozievents.com

How to apply:
>Email your headshot and resume to
>Jimmy@scoozievents.com and he'll let
>you know when they have their next
>open call.

http://twitter.com/scoozievents
http://www.facebook.com/pages/Scoozi-
Events/146939375350264
http://www.linkedin.com/company/scoozi-
events-nyc

Top Shelf Staffers

Phone: (212) 842-1033
Website: http://topshelfstaffers.com

How to apply:
Online at:
http://topshelfstaffers.com/employment.
aspx

http://twitter.com/TopShelfStaff
http://www.facebook.com/pages/Top-Shelf-
Staffing/110042545718358

Temp:

While I went over some interview tips in the beginning, I thought I'd share a few more tips to help you put your best foot forward for your temp interview, since it is a little more formal than a promo or catering interview.

* Ideally have your resume printed out on resume paper. You can get this at any office supply store.

* Bring 2 forms of ID – this is usually your Social Security card and your Driver's License, or your Passport.

* They'll have you fill out an I-9 and a W-4 form; you've probably seen these dozens of times, ask the receptionist if you have any questions on how to fill them out.

* Gather your forms of ID, print your resumes, iron/steam your clothes, and pack your bag the night before so you don't have to scramble around the morning of to get everything together.

* Make a cheat sheet for yourself for these applications – they're basically all the same. At one office I had to give at least 3 co-worker reference names & phone numbers along with the

50

addresses and phone numbers of my last 3 employers.

* Plan on getting to the temp office at least 15 minutes early. You'll probably have to sign-in with the security desk in the building lobby (there's always a line if you're running late.) Also, you'll have to fill out a bunch of paperwork before you meet the temp agent.

* Dress professionally. If you don't have a suit, wear a pair of black pants and a button-up shirt. Please make sure you iron or steam your clothes before you go. I always wear tennis shoes around the city, but I change into my nice dress shoes before I get off the subway and stash my tennies in my bag (but make sure to zip it up.) I use a computer bag that looks like a nice bag, but still has room to hold my portfolio and tennis shoes.

* Get yourself a nice, plain folder, or a portfolio (with a pocket) for interviews. This will keep your resume nice and clean, and give you space to write down any questions you may have.

* When you meet the temp agent, offer a handshake and smile! She will probably ask you for your resume first

thing, so have that ready to give to her, don't spend a few minutes shuffling through your bags to get it.

* The temp agent will usually say "Tell me a little about your experience" – have about a minute overview of your office work ready – or if you haven't done office work before, just talk about what experience you do have. It helps to have a copy of your resume in front of you as you talk, so you can refer to different items on it.

* While you're in the meeting ask what is the best way to keep in contact with the temp agent / how do they want you to keep them updated with your availability? Each office is different, but usually an email once a week with your availability for the next week is useful.

* You'll probably have to do some computer tests; typing, Microsoft Word, Excel, etc. If you're not too familiar with these programs check out the free tutorials. I would start with Office 2007: http://office.microsoft.com/en-us/training-FX101782702.aspx Doing all of the computer tests usually makes the interview last a couple of hours, so be prepared to be there for a while.

* After you go home, shoot them a nice little email, or send a hand-written thank you – something like:

> "It was a pleasure to meet with you today. Thanks for taking the time to share with me the (insert temp agency name here) process. I look forward to working together" (and so on.)

Access Staffing

Phone: (212) 687-5440
Website: http://accessstaffing.com

How to apply:
>   Email your resume to Althea:
>   Adennis@accessstaffing.com

http://twitter.com/AccessStaffing
http://www.linkedin.com/company/access-staffing

Addison Group

Phone: (646) 385-7877
Website: http://www.addisonsearch.com

How to apply:
    Email your resume to:
    angelina.coloma@addisongroup.com

http://www.linkedin.com/company/addison-search

Adecco

Phone: (212) 391-7000
http://www.adeccousa.com

How to apply:
Submit your resume via their website:
http://www.adeccousa.com/Pages/Passi
veApply.aspx

Note from Survival Jobs: Adecco does
Hospitality & Office Staffing. If you are
interested in both, you can submit your
resume for one (whichever you think your
resume is strongest for) and when you go in
for your interview indicate that you're
interested in both.

http://twitter.com/adeccousa
http://www.facebook.com/Adecco
http://www.linkedin.com/company/adecco
http://www.youtube.com/adeccousa

AppleOne Employment Services

Phone: (212) 697-6770
Website: http://www.appleone.com

How to apply:
   Apply online:
   https://www.appleone.com/OnlineApplic
   ation/ola_contact.aspx

http://www.facebook.com/pages/AppleOne-
Employment-Services/30583971214

Atrium Staffing

Phone: (212) 292-0550
Website: http://www.atriumstaff.com

How to apply:
Email your resume to Sara:
sboller@atriumstaff.com

Note from Survival Jobs: I know, as with children, you're not supposed to have favorites. But Atrium has always received great feedback from my actors and they placed me in a great temp gig.

http://twitter.com/atriumstaff
http://www.facebook.com/AtriumStaffing
http://www.linkedin.com/company/atrium-staffing

BON TEMPS

Phone: (212) 732-3921
Website: http://bontempsny.com

How to apply:
Email your resume (in word and pdf formats – if you have it) to:
beatrice@bontempsny.com

Note from Survival Jobs: BON TEMPS is primarily a legal staffing office, although they do occasionally use general admin temps as well.

Career Group Inc.

Phone: (212) 750-8188
Website: http://careergroupinc.com

How to apply:
Email your resume to:
cginy@careergroupinc.com

http://twitter.com/careergroupinc

Clarity Staffing

Phone: (212) 404-8000
Website: http://www.claritystaffing.com

How to apply:
    Online at:
    http://www.claritystaffing.com/submit-your-resume

http://twitter.com/ClarityStaffing
http://www.facebook.com/ClarityLLC

Core Staffing

Phone: (212) 766-1222
Website: http://employcore.com

How to apply:
> Email temp@employcore.com. Attach your resume as a word document and write a short paragraph outlining your ability.

http://twitter.com/corestaffingny
http://www.linkedin.com/company/core-staffing

First Choice Staffing

Phone: (646) 536-5600
Website: http://www.firstchoicestaffingny.com

How to apply:
> Email resumes@firstchoiceny.com with "Survival Jobs for Actors" in the subject line. Attach your resume as an MS Word document.

Gainor Staffing

Phone: (212) 697-4145
Website: http://www.gainor.net

How to apply:
> Online at:
> http://gainorjobs.haleymarketing.com/template.smpl?arg=jb_user_signup

http://twitter.com/Gainor_HR

Glocap

Phone: (212) 333-6400
Website: http://www.glocap.com

How to apply:
>Email your resume to Caitlin Hafner:
>Hafner@glocap.com

Note from Survival Jobs: Glocap is a giant in the finance industry. If you have a suit, this is definitely the interview to wear it.
(Another one of my favorite companies.)

http://twitter.com/glocap
http://www.linkedin.com/company/glocap-search

Hudson Gate Partners

Phone: (212) 763-8481
Website: http://www.hudsongatepartners.com

How to apply:
    Send your resume to:
    jobs@hudsongatepartners.com detailing
    what type of look you're working for.

http://twitter.com/HudsonGate
http://www.linkedin.com/company/hudson-gate-partners

Jennifer Temps

Phone: (212) 964-8367
Website: http://www.jennifertemps.com/

How to apply:
>Email: resumes@jennifertemps.com. In the subject line, write the type of work you're looking for. Attach your resume as a word document.

Kaye Personnel (New Jersey)

Phone: (856) 489-1010
Website: http://www.kayepersonnel.com

How to apply:
> Email your resume to
> cherryhillstaff@kayepersonnel.com.
> Note that you are looking for temp work.

Kelly Services

Phone: (212) 949-8545
Website: http://www.kellyservices.com

How to apply:
Online at:
https://kellycareernetwork.tms.hrdepart
ment.com/cgi-
bin/a/editprofile.cgi?jobid=&referralsourc
e=&job_referer=&job_referreruid=&raf=

http://twitter.com/KellyServices
http://www.facebook.com/kellyservices
http://www.linkedin.com/company/kellyservice
s

Lang Staffing Partners

Phone: (212) 683-0831 x105
Website: http://www.langnyc.com

How to apply:
      Email Louis Irizarry: li@langnyc.com

http://www.facebook.com/pages/Lang-Staffing-Partners/215604718467508

Llyod Staffing

Phone: (212) 551-1020
Website: http://www.lloydstaffing.com

How to apply:
      Email your resume in Word to:
      dawnv@lloydstaffing.com.

http://twitter.com/lloydstaffing
http://www.facebook.com/lloydstaffingli
http://www.linkedin.com/company/lloyd-staffing

Metropolitan Staffing Services

Phone: (212) 983-6060
Website: http://www.metstaff.com

How to apply:
MEsposito@metstaff.com

Note from Survival Jobs: They also have a hospitality division (Met Hospitality.) If you are interested in that as well, be sure to mention it. From time to time they get promo gigs, so feel free to include your headshot if that's something you want to be considered for. But, if you are submitting your business resume just for temp work, no need to send in a picture.

PeopleFinders Plus

Phone: (212) 953-3772
Website: http://www.peoplefindersplus.com

How to apply:
    Email your resume to:
    jess@peoplefindersplus.com

Note from Survival Jobs: Jessica is a huge fan of Survival Jobs and loves the actors she finds through us.

Professionals for NonProfits (PNP)

Phone: (212) 546-9091
Website: http://nonprofitstaffing.com

How to apply:
>   Online at:
>   https://eoffice.nonprofitstaffing.com/ebiz/php/app-general.php

http://twitter.com/NYPNP
http://www.facebook.com/pages/Professionals-for-NonProfits/132303730848
http://www.linkedin.com/company/professionals-for-nonprofits

Taylor Hodson

Phone: (212) 924-8300
Website: http://www.taylorhodson.com

How to apply:
    Email your resume to:
    tempjob@taylorhodson.com

http://twitter.com/taylorhodson
http://www.facebook.com/pages/Taylor-
Hodson-Staffing/172101254975

Temporary Staffing by Suzanne

Phone: (212) 856-9500
Website: http://suzannenyc.com

How to apply:
Email your resume to:
info@suzannenyc.com; or fax it to (212)
856-4426.

Tempositions

Phone: (212) 490-7400
Website: http://www.tempositions.com

How to apply:
>   Online at:
>   http://www.tempositions.com/site/work.a
>   spx

http://twitter.com/tempositions
http://www.facebook.com/tempositions
http://www.linkedin.com/company/the-
tempositions-group-of-companies

The Supporting Cast

Phone: (212) 532-8888
Website: http://www.supportingcast.com

How to apply:
>Email your resume to Maria:
>mmileva@supportingcast.com

Note from Survival Jobs: The Supporting Cast also has a hospitality division. If you're interested in that as well, be sure to mention it.

http://twitter.com/castny
http://www.facebook.com/pages/The-Supporting-Cast/253898798624
http://www.linkedin.com/company/78602?trk=tyah

The Tuttle Agency

Phone: (212) 497-9500
Website: http://www.tuttleagency.com

How to apply:
> Online at:
> http://www.tuttleagency.com/submitresume.asp

Working with Children:

NYC Nanny Finder
Phone: (646) 660-2401
Website: http://www.nycnannyfinder.com

How to apply:
>Online – submit the application on their website:
http://www.nycnannyfinder.com/nannys_lounge/candidate_register.php

http://twitter.com/nycnannyfinder
http://www.youtube.com/user/nycnannyfinder
https://plus.google.com/108681736318379370149/posts

Little Maestros

Phone: (212) 396-3977
Website: http://littlemaestros.com

How to apply:
> Email your headshot and resume to:
> casting@littlemaestros.com

Note from Little Maestros: "Available positions include Male Lead/Guitarist, Female Vocalist, Pianist, and Drummer."

http://www.facebook.com/littlemaestros

NY Kids Club

Phone: (347) 706-4700
Website: http://www.nykidsclub.com

How to apply:
Check out their website at:
http://www.nykidsclub.com/careers.cfm

http://twitter.com/newyorkkidsclub
http://www.facebook.com/newyorkkidsclub
http://www.linkedin.com/company/2365599?tr
k=jobtocomp

Fitness:

There are many certification programs to become a personal trainer or instructor. Here are a few of the most widely accepted programs. (Be sure to check with wherever you want to apply to see what certification they accept before you pay to take the course.)

* NASM - www.nasm.org

* ACE - www.acefitness.org

* ISSA - www.issaonline.com

Quick overview - you buy the materials from the company, learn them on your own, then take the test. Most of the tests are computer based, and you can find a testing center on their website.

Some programs have a weekend class or personal training workshop that you can take. It's a good way to get hands-on training from professionals that have already been through the process.

You also need CPR certification to get your personal trainer certification. Go to www.RedCross.org to find a CPR class in your area. Type in your area code, go to your local Red Cross' website to check class schedules.

When you work for a large gym, at the beginning, you are required to work floor hours – which means hanging around on the floor to answer questions and help the members with machines.

24 Hour Fitness

Phone: 1-800-224-0240
Website: http://www.24hourfitness.com

How to apply:
http://www.24hourfitness.com/company/careers

http://twitter.com/24hourfitness
http://www.facebook.com/24HourFitness
http://www.linkedin.com/company/24-hour-fitness
http://www.youtube.com/user/24HourFitnessInc

Beachbody

Website:
http://www.GetFitMakeMoneyBeHappy.com

What it is:

Beachbody is a health and fitness company that offers such programs as P90X, Turbo Jam, Insanity, and Shakeology. Become a coach and sell their products via your website and encourage others to better their life through health and fitness. You do not need to have a fitness certification for this gig. It's a business you can do completely on your own schedule, and from anywhere. Plus, you get discounts on their products. Check out the website above for more information.

How to apply:

Email Michelle at DyerFitness@gmail.com with a little bit about yourself and why you're interested in this opportunity.

http://www.twitter.com/DyerFitness
http://www.facebook.com/DyerFitness
http://www.pinterest.com/DyerFitness

Equinox

Phone: (212) 677-0180
Website: http://www.equinox.com

How to apply:
    http://www.equinox.com/classic/Careers
    .aspx

Note from Survival Jobs: Equinox also has
their own personal training program.
http://www.equinox.com/education/personaltra
ining

https://twitter.com/Equinox
http://www.facebook.com/Equinox
http://www.linkedin.com/company/equinox
http://www.youtube.com/user/equinox

New York Sports Clubs (NYSC)

Website:
http://www.mysportsclubs.com/regions/NYSC.htm?WT.svl=Header

How to apply:
>
> Online at:
> https://wfa.kronostm.com/index.jsp?applicationName=TownSportsNonReqExt&locale=en_US

http://www.facebook.com/MySportsClubs
http://www.linkedin.com/company/town-sports-international

Restaurant Groups:

Bowlmor
Phone: (212) 255-8188
Website: http://www.bowlmor.com

How to apply:
> Stop by 110 University Place to fill out an application or submit your resume to jobs@bowlmor.com. Be sure to mention the position you are applying for (i.e. Server, Bartender, Front Desk/ Host) and the location.

http://twitter.com/bowlmorlanes
http://www.facebook.com/BowlmorLanes
http://www.linkedin.com/company/bowlmor-lanes

B.R. Guest

Phone: (212) 209-8903
Website: http://www.brguesthospitality.com

How to apply:
Email your resume to
careers@brguestinc.com or apply online
at
http://www.brguesthospitality.com/caree
rs

Note from Survival Jobs: This is a huge
hospitality group that includes Dos Caminos,
Blue Fin, and Ruby Foo's Times Square.

http://twitter.com/brghospitality
http://www.facebook.com/BRGuestHospitality
http://www.linkedin.com/company/br-guest

Fireman Hospitality Group

Phone: (212) 399-1325
Website: http://thefhg.com

How to apply:
> Physically go to one of their restaurants and fill out an application on site, or email your resume to Danielle at DBucci@thefiremangroup.com.

http://www.linkedin.com/company/the-fireman-hospitality-group

Bartending Classes:

These Bartending Schools help place students after you take their class.

ABC Bartending School

Phone: (212) 594-4146
Website: http://abcbartending.com

Classes:

    Their 40 hour class is $395. There are different schedules where you can take the class; all in one week, part-time, weekends, etc. They do placements for bars that call in to request employees, and for private parties. Actors are usually requested for the private parties. Call (212) 594-4146 to register for the class in midtown.

Barnard Bartending Agency

Phone: (212) 854-4650
Website: http://www.barnardbartending.com

Where to find out about classes:
   http://www.barnardbartending.com/stud
   ents

http://twitter.com/barnardbartend

Broadway Merchandise:

Marquee Merchandise

Phone: (212) 529-5810
Website: http://marqueemerchandise.com

How to apply:
> Quote from Marquee "If you see any listings on Playbill.com you can apply."

The Araca Group

Website: http://www.araca.com

How to apply:
> Send your resume to hiring@araca.com and mention that you're interested in selling merchandise.

http://twitter.com/TheAracaGroup
http://www.facebook.com/TheAracaGroup?v=app_392248091048&ref=ts
http://www.linkedin.com/company/the-araca-group

Broadway Concessions:

Sweet Concessions
(also 212-Events)
Phone: (212) 582-5472
Website: http://www.sweetconcessions.com

How to apply:
> Stop by their office and fill out an
> application.
> 1650 Broadway, Suite 510

Note from Survival Jobs: 212-Events also does catering.

http://www.facebook.com/pages/Sweet-Concessions/117866549027
http://www.facebook.com/pages/212-EVENTS/124875394213715

Theatre Refreshment Company

Phone: (212) 586-7610
Website: http://www.theatrerefreshment.com

How to apply:
> Stop by their office and fill out an
> application – bring your resume.
> 346 W. 44th Street

http://twitter.com/theatrerefresh
http://www.facebook.com/TheatreRefreshmen
t
http://www.linkedin.com/company/theatre-
refreshment-company

Tour Guide:

On Location Tours

Phone: (212) 683-2027
Website: http://www.screentours.com

How to apply:
    Email a headshot and resume to
    marketing@onlocationtours.com

http://twitter.com/onlocationtours
http://www.facebook.com/onlocationtoursnyc

Real Estate:

Rapid NYC

Phone: (347) 404-5202
Website: http://www.rapidnyc.com

How to apply:
 Details online at:
http://www.rapidnyc.com/careers/apply

Note from Survival Jobs: For more information on working in Real Estate check out their great FAQ page:
http://www.rapidnyc.com/careers/faq

http://twitter.com/rapidrealtynyc
http://www.facebook.com/rapidrealty
http://www.linkedin.com/company/rapid-realty
http://www.youtube.com/user/RapidRealtyVid
eos

Telesales:

Roundabout Theatre Company
Phone: (212) 719-9393
Website: http://www.roundabouttheatre.org

How to apply:
> Call 212-642-9625 Ext. 8200 to
> schedule an interview.

Note from Survival Jobs:
> This job is for ticket sales for
> Roundabout's season, so the months of
> work may vary. This is a Monday –
> Friday, 5:00pm – 9:00pm job.

http://twitter.com/rtc_nyc
http://www.facebook.com/RoundaboutTheatre
Company
http://www.linkedin.com/company/roundabout-
theatre-
companyhttp://www.youtube.com/rtc10018

Broadway.com/Theatre Direct International

Phone: (212) 541-8457
Website: http://www.broadway.com

How to apply:

> Send a resume and cover letter to:
> hr@broadway.com. Include your current
> employment, or most recent
> employment, as well as your salary
> history and expectations.

<u>Bonus:</u>

To download a spreadsheet to help you keep track of what jobs you've applied for, go here:

http://www.survivaljobsforactors.com/nyc_bonus_here

On the same page, you can sign up for our email list to keep in touch with us!

Other helpful resources:

www.SurvivalJobsForActors.com

www.TheBestSurvivalJob.com

www.ResourcesForActors.com

www.SubletsForActors.com

Follow us on Twitter:
@SurvivalJobs

www.ingramcontent.com/pod-product-compliance
Lightning Source LLC
Chambersburg PA
CBHW071619040426
42452CB00009B/1402